Let's Choose Our Worship

A GUIDE FOR THOSE LEADING WORSHIP

THE SAINT ANDREW PRESS
EDINBURGH

First Published in 1980 by
THE SAINT ANDREW PRESS
121 George Street, Edinburgh

Reprinted 1981, 1982, 1983

Copyright © The Woman's Guild of
The Church of Scotland, 1980

ISBN 0 7152 0461 0

All rights reserved. No part of this publication may be reproduced or transmitted in any form or by any means, electronic or mechanical, including photocopy, recording, or any information storage or retrieval system, without permission in writing from the publisher. This book is sold subject to the condition that it shall not, by way of trade or otherwise, be lent, re-sold, hired out or otherwise circulated without the publisher's prior consent.

Printed in Great Britain by
SUNPrint, Glasgow Road, Dumfries.

CONTENTS

	PAGE
Introduction	5
The Singing	7
The Reading	7
Helpful Bible Readings	8
The Prayer	9
Adoration	11
Confession	13
Supplication	15
Thanksgiving	17
Intercession	19
Well-known Prayers	21
Some Prayers from around the World	23
Prayers for Special Meetings	25
A Home Mission Meeting	25
An Overseas Meeting	27
A Social Responsibilty Meeting	29
A Young Woman's Group	31
A Committee Meeting	33
An Annual General Meeting	34

INTRODUCTION

Worship in the Woman's Guild is the main activity which makes the Guild different from many other women's meetings. To conduct the devotions is a wonderful privilege but also a big responsibility. In worship we acknowledge Almighty God as Creator and Lord of all; we share our love for our Lord Jesus Christ; and together, in the Spirit, leader and people, we seek both His pardon and His blessing.

It would be impossible to produce a pattern of worship which would meet the need of all Guild branches for they are so different. It is usual for devotions to come at the beginning of a meeting but this need not always be so. There is no set PATTERN of worship which must be followed, so try to develop your own form, your own pattern, for each occasion. Vary them so that the devotions don't become set in one form. Try an epilogue occasionally. Tying all the thoughts of a meeting together with a closing act of worship can be very effective.

Whatever you decide, take time beforehand to plan your act of worship, so that hymn, reading and prayer are linked together around the theme of your meeting.

Leading the worship is not the sole responsibility of the president. Use the office-bearers and others. Perhaps two or three could share this part of the meeting. Involve as many Guild members as possible.

THE SINGING

Singing is one way of expressing our feelings. If you decide to open your meeting with a hymn, be sure it is one which is well known, so that your meeting gets off to a good start. Make sure the pianist has been told of your choice and whether or not you sing 'Amen'.

Don't restrict your singing to hymns alone and don't be afraid to try something different. Many Guilds have their own favourite humns (and their own hymnbooks!) but there are many songs which are not to be found in the hymnary which express what we want to say and which are well known, e.g. 'Amazing Grace', 'What a friend we have in Jesus', 'How great Thou art', 'When I needed a neighbour', and so on. Many such hymns are to be found in the following song books which can be obtained from the Church of Scotland bookshops:

    Youth Praise 1   Sing to God
    Youth Praise 2   Sound of Living Waters

It may well be that your church already has these books of praise. Ask your organist about this posibility.

Many well-known hymns can be sung to secular tunes if you want something different. Two such examples are Hymn 451 (CH3) 'Almightly Father of all things that be'. Usual tune - Chilton Foliat. Suggested tune - Now is the Hour. Hymn 390 (CH3) 'O greatly blessed Thy people are'. Usual tune - St Stephen. Suggested tune - The Northern Lights of Old Aberdeen.

THE READING

Having chosen the hymn or song, try to find a reading that will link up with the theme of the meeting. This need not be from the Bible on every occasion. If there is a relevant passage then of course use it, but do not hesitate to use a poem or passage from a book or magazine, if it says what you want to say. Keep a watchful eye when you are reading magazines for snippets which could be useful. Cut them out and keep them in a scrapbook for the time you want to use them. There are many books by writers such as Rita Snowden, Beryl Bye, Helen Steiner Rice, all of which contain a wide range of material which can be used as readings.

"Spotlight", the magazine produced by representatives from the Church of Scotland Woman's Guild, Home Mission, Social Responsibility and Overseas Women's Councils, together with the Education Department, also carries a devotional page which could be used on an appropriate occasion. The Theme Brochure too has a page devoted to helpful books. Have you thought of building up your own Guild Branch library of devotional material? This would be helpful to any member of the Guild who is asked to take the devotions.

Whatever reading you decide upon, study it beforehand so that you can read it at the meeting, putting in the proper emphasis, and not faltering over any unfamiliar words. Read it slowly and distinctly. Remember that your listeners do not have the words in front of them, and depend on you to make the meaning clear to them. Make sure your reading is not too long.

Sometimes the speaker (if you have one) likes a special passage to be read. Check on this when reminding her/him of the meeting, and be sure to be familiar with it before the meeting. This means you can face your task with assurance, because you are prepared.

HELPFUL BIBLE READINGS
The Beautitudes - Matthew 5 v 3-10
The Parable of the Good Samaritan - Luke 10 v 25-37
The Prodigal Son - Luke 15 v 11-32
The Raising of Lazarus - John 11 v 1-44
Feeding of the Five Thousand - Luke 9 v 10-17
Healing of Jairus' daughter - Luke 8 v 40-56
The Transfiguration of Christ - Luke 9 v 28-36
The Calming of the storm - Mark 4 v 35-41
The Calling of the Disciples - Luke 5 v 1-11; Luke 6 v 12-16
The Temptations in the Wilderness - Luke 4 v 1-14
The Parable of the Sower - Matthew 13 v 1-9
Jesus' Teaching on Prayer - Luke 11 v 1-13
Trust in God - Luke 12 v 22-34
Jesus and Zacchaeus - Luke 19 v 1-10
The Wedding in Cana - John 2 v 1-12
Jesus and the Samaritan Woman - John 4 v 1-42
The Triumphant Entry into Jerusalem - Luke 19 v 28-40
The Last Supper -
The Garden of Gethsemane -   } John 13-21
The Trial of Jesus -
The Crucifixion and Resurrection -

The Coming of the Holy Spirit - Acts 2 v 1-42
The Story of Lydia - Acts 16 v 11-15
Life in God's Service - Romans 12 v 1-21
Love - 1 Corinthians 13 v 1-13
One Body with Many Parts - 1 Corinthians 12 v 12-31; Ephesians 4 v 1-6
Wives and Husbands

Ephesians 5 v 21-33;
Children and Parents   Ephesians 6 v 1-4
The Whole Armour of God - Ephesians 6 v 10-18
The Parable of the Sheep and the Goats - Matthew 25 v 31-46
Christ's Promise to be with us always - Matthew 28 v 16-20

THE PRAYER

Leading in prayer is perhaps the most demanding and difficult part of the devotions, but prayer is simply talking to God. Use your own language if not using a traditional prayer, for this will be more readily understood by those you seek to lead. People just do not listen if the prayers are too long, so make them short and meaningful for all who are present.

It is sometimes helpful before prayer to **draw attention** to the main themes in it - e.g. "On this Overseas night we shall be praying for the work in India, for our missionary partner, for a deeper understanding of mission by those of us at home. Now let us pray . . .".

Two essentials for any prayer are sincerity and simplicity. You will find it helpful to write down your prayer as you plan it. Prayer can be divided into the following sections:

1. Adoration — responding to God's presence, we bow before His greatness and goodness.
2. Confession (saying sorry) — thinking of God, we are aware of our own faults and failings.
3. Supplication (asking) — we ask for God's help to overcome our failings and to be made more like Him.
4. Thanksgiving — we give thanks for all God's goodness to us.

5. Intercession (asking for help for others) — we pray for others and ask God's help for them.

It is not necessary to include every section in every prayer, but using them as a guide does help you not to go round in circles! When planning your prayer, think of your fellow Guild members and their needs; think of the meeting and the message you are trying to pass on - think of your Heavenly Father who will be with you in it all.

The following pages contain sentence prayers under the five sections already listed on the previous page. These short prayers are designed to help you make up your own prayers. Alter and adapt any of these suggestions to fit your own need. Perhaps you have members who are sick at home or in hospital and would like to mention them. Perhaps you would want to pray for your Sunday School and teachers. Use the appropriate sentence prayer and make it your own.

Also included are some old, traditional prayers, together with some new prayers which you might find helpful. There are prayers for special meetings too.

"Pray Today" contains many suitable prayers for use in Guild meetings, as does Spotlight and the Theme Booklet. Other helpful books are:

A Woman's Book of Prayers — Rita Snowden
More Prayers for Women — Rita Snowden
Short Prayers for the Long Day — Giles and Melville Harcourt (Collins)
Daily Praise and Prayer — George Appleton
A Chain of Prayer across the Ages — Selina Fox
A Diary of Private Prayer — John Baillie

For further suggestions, see revised and re-printed sheet — "Guidelines for Worship".

ADORATION
Drawing near to God and thinking of Him

There are various ways of commencing the prayer: "Let us pray...."; "Now our prayer...."; "Now we pray together..." — having invited all to join in prayer, allow a little pause so that all can turn their thoughts to God.

———

Our God and our Father,
Everything we have and are comes from You.
We marvel at Your love and so we come to worship You.

———

Loving Lord, we come to You with joy and gratitude.
Your sending Jesus into the world has made all the difference to our lives —
All the difference between darkness and light.

———

Living, Loving God,
The beauty of Your world speaks to us of Your love.
We come to You humbly and full of praise and thankfulness.

———

Almighty God, You are all-powerful and all-knowing.
When we remember this we are amazed that You should love us.
We rejoice because we know this is true.

———

Lord, it is evening and we come to You for Your blessing.
We would be quiet and still in your presence and draw peace from You.

Dear God and Father,
In love you created us and set us in a world of beauty.
We come joyfully to worship and praise You.

———

Almighty God, Creator of all things,
We worship You in the stillness of this evening hour.
The world about us speaks to us of Your greatness.
We marvel and rejoice that You are our Father.

———

Loving lord, we come to worship You.
You know each one of us and just how much we need
   You.

———

CONFESSION
Seeing ourselves in God's Light

We ask forgiveness for the many ways in which we limit our lives,
—by failing to see the beauty around us
—by failing to help others
—by forgetting that there is much more to life than our daily tasks and rising prices
—by trying to live in our own strength

———

Forgive us, Lord, that we have not loved others as You have loved us.
So often we have put our own pleasures and comforts before the needs of others.

———

Lord, we confess that we have listened to gossip and enjoyed it.
Forgive us and give us the courage to refuse to listen, trying only to see the good there is in others.

———

Lord, forgive us that we have not yet wholly trusted You.
We have been anxious about many things this day and failed to see the needs of others.

———

We have forgotten that Your love surrounds us at all times.

———

Father, forgive our lack of faith.
You have called us to love and trust You, but today we have been so concerned with the material things of this life that we have neglected You.

Dear Lord, in Your presence we see ourselves as we are, showing so little of Your love and concern for others.
Forgive us and help us to live more closely to You that we may be more like You.

———

Loving Lord, forgive us that we have taken You for granted today.
We have enjoyed every good thing that You have sent and failed to realise that these are tokens of Your love.
Help us always to remember that all we have comes from You.

———

SUPPLICATION
Asking for God's help to meet our needs

Dear Lord, we come to You as we are,
    some joyful, others sad,
    some contented, others anxious and afraid,
    speak to us in our several needs.
    Help us to look beyond ourselves to see the needs of others.
    Help us to know Your love each day is with us.

———

Father, give us love, love which does not count the cost of giving,
    love which knows no barriers,
    love like that of our Saviour Christ.

———

Almighty God, help us to understand prayer as living contact with You,
    help us to be open to Your guidance
    Help us to follow Your leading even when we cannot see where that will lead us. Give us faith to follow.

———

Living Lord, You are with us and in us;
wherever we are, You will be there too.
Accept our thanks for the promise of Your presence.
Help us to live as those who know Your forgiving love.
May Your joy and peace be seen in our lives.

———

Loving Lord, guide our thoughts,
    guide our words.

    guide our actions,
    that all we think and speak and do may
    be to Your glory.

———

Father, give us light, to recognise Your presence in
       ordinary everyday things,
       to help us with the problems
       we have to face,
       to bring happiness and understanding to others.

———

Dear Lord, help us in our singing and praying,
    in our listening and speaking,
    to offer You the joy of our whole being,
    and the dedication of our lives.

———

Almighty God, our lord and King,
Help us to know You are with us all the day long.
Help us to know You care about what happens to us.
Help us to know that nothing can take Your love from us.

———

THANKSGIVING
Giving thanks for all God's goodness

Dear Lord, we thank You for Your love
seen so clearly through the life of Christ our Saviour;
and for the assurance that Your love will never die.

———

Lord, we thank You for our warm comfortable homes.
Be with those who are away from home —
         in hostels
         in lodgings
         in shared flats
Especially be near to those sleeping rough, without
  homes of their own. Thank You for places like the
  People's Palace and Kirkhaven.
Bless all who work there.

———

Creator God, we thank You for the beauty of the
         earth,
         for the changing seasons, each with its
         own loveliness;
         for the song of the birds and the sheer
         joy of living.

———

Father, we thank You for Your Loving patience with us.
Often we take Your love for granted without even a
  "thank you".
We cannot understand why You love us Lord, but thank
  You
for Christ's message of Your forgiving, transforming
  love.
Make us channels of that love to our families and those
  with whom we come into contact every day.

Dear Lord, we thank You for the fellowhship we have within our Guild.
We are so different, yet we all matter to You.
Thank you for Your love which unites us.
Thank You for calling us into Your service.

———

Thank you, Lord, for the joy and happiness we find in Your service,
for the caring, and sharing work of our church,
for the privilege of being a part of it.

———

Almighty God, we than You for all that makes our lives so full and happy;
for our homes and those whom we love;
for our Guild and the friendship we find within it;
for our church and the opportunity of service;
for the community in which we live and the warm sense of belonging which it gives.
Help us always to be ready to share with others the sense of purpose which these blessings bring.

———

INTERCESSION
Asking God's help and blessing for others

We pray for all absent members,
may Your blessing be upon them wherever they are.
May they know we are thinking of them,
may they know themselves to be a real part of our fellowship.

―――

We bring to You those of our members who are anxious and afraid,
some are concerned for ageing parents,
some are anxious for children living away from home.
You know the things which worry us, Lord
Help us to share these burdens with You, and to know Your support at all times.

―――

We pray for all who carry the reponsibility of leadership.
Give them wisdom and a clear understanding of what is best for all.
Help us all to be ready to take our share of responsibility within our Guild and Community.

―――

We pray for all elderly people:
      for those who feel their years a burden,
      for those who are confused in mind, or frail in body;
      for those who feel alone and unwanted,
      for those who feel no one cares.
Help us to see our responsibility for all these people, dear Lord.
Help us to show them Your love by caring for them.

―――

We pray for those who are ill at home or in hospital,

thinking particularly of those known to us;
give them courage and patience,
help them to know that they are always within Your love.
Help us to see more clearly our part in caring for them.

―――

Almighty God, whose love is for all mankind,
bless the work of those agencies which seek to bring help to those who suffer because of war and violence, hatred and fear.
In our land of plenty, help us to remember the needs of the refugees and those who haven't enough food to eat.

―――

WELL-KNOWN PRAYERS

Almighty God, unto whom all hearts be open,
all desires known and from whom no secrets are hid.
cleanse the thoughts of our hearts
by the inspiration of Thy Holy Spirit,
that we may perfectly love Thee and
Worthily magnify Thy Holy Name.

———

Teach us, good Lord,
to serve Thee as Thou deservest,
to give, and not to count the cost,
to fight and not to heed the wounds,
to toil and not to seek for rest,
to labour and not to ask for any reward
Save that of knowing that we do Thy will.

———

Lighten our darkness, we beseech Thee, O Lord,
and by Thy great mercy defend us from all perils and
    and dangers of this night,
For the love of Thy only son, our Saviour Jesus Christ.

———

God be in my head, and in my understanding,
God be in mine eyes and in my looking,
God be in my mouth and in my speaking,
God be in my heart and in my thinking,
God be at mine end and at my departing.

———

Lord, make us instruments of Thy peace.
Where there is hatred, let us sow love,
where there is injury, pardon,
where there is discord, union,
where there is doubt, faith,
where there is despair, hope
where there is darkness, light.

where there is sadness, joy,
for Thy mercy and for Thy truth's sake, Amen.

O God, forasmuch as without Thee,
we are not able to please Thee,
mercifully grant that Thy Holy Spirit
may in all things direct and rule our hearts.

SOME PRAYERS FROM AROUND THE WORLD

O God, we worship and praise You for Your great love to us,
we know that You desire only our highest good;
may we ever seek to walk humbly in Your appointed way for us,
binding ourselves to You in living and constant obedience.

(Brigalia Bam — W.C.C.)

———

Grant us peace beyond our present understanding.
Supply us with compassion, kindness, humility, gentleness and patience.
Help us exercise forbearance and forgiveness for others,
through Jesus Christ our Lord, Amen.

(Margaret Shannon — U.S.A.)

———

We thank You, dear Heavenly Father, that we can come to You with all our difficulties, and claim Your offered peace.
Help each one to remember this and to take it.
To every troubled soul grant healing peace,
through our Lord and Saviour, Jesus Christ, Amen.

(Rosemary McNeill — West Indies)

———

Lord, give us the courage to accept the risks of loving and self-giving,
so that through our love for each other we may encounter You,
the source of all love.

(E. Lovatt-Dolan — W.U.C.W.)

Dear father, bless our children.
Give us understanding of them,
Tenderness and patience with them.
May we find joy in them and they in us.
May they grow up to know Your love and to response to it with all their hearts.

———

Lord Jesus Christ, we have so little to offer You,
but we rejoice in the promises You have made to us.
You have been hurt by our lack of faith,
yet we trust in Your unfailing grace, in Your power to seek and find us afresh,
Your power to keep us in Your love and Your power to re-kindle our faith again and again.
Send us back into the world with new vision, new strength, new love, new hope and new faith.
(Theme Booklet - 1979-80)

———

PRAYERS FOR SPECIAL MEETINGS

Prayer for a Home Mission meeting

Make still our hearts before You, O God, that we may worship You in Spirit and in Faith.

Let us unite in prayer:
Heavenly Father, earth is full of Your majesty and glory.
We are so small and insignificant, yet we would offer to You our praise and adoration.
We thank You for your goodness to us — for all the pleasant things in our lives: the joys of friendship, of family life.
We thank You for all those who have served You in the past, and now rejoice in Your nearer Presence.

We ask for Your forgiveness for all we have done that falls short of Your example.
We admit that, though we try to be strong for You, we are beset by human failings — help us, we ask You, and guide us in Your ways.

We would commend to Your care, all those who work to further Your Kingdom here on earth,
especially we think of all Deacons, Deaconesses and Lay Missionaries.
Be with them every day — guide them, and guard them, and grant that they may see some reward for their labours.

We would ask Your blessing on all who are sick or handicapped in mind or body;
lay Your healing hand upon them and comfort them.

Help us, O Heavenly Father, to place others before self
 and to use such gifts as we may have to their best
 advantage.
Help us to remember that You are always with us.
Especially, help us to listen, so that, in hearing what
 others say, we may seek to help them.

We listen for Your message, O God.
Enter into our hearts, and grant us Your peace.
Amen.

Prayers for an Overseas Meeting

God, our Father, as we seek to follow the example of our Lord Jesus Christ in working and praying that Your Kingdom may come, Your will be done on earth, we need the guidance of Your Holy Spirit.

Give us, Father, a vision of Your world as love would make it:

a world where the weak are protected and none go hungry;

a world whose benefits are shared so that everyone can enjoy them;

a world whose different people and cultures live with tolerance and mutual respect;

a world where peace is built with justice and justice is fired with love.

And give us, and all with whom we are joined in the Fellowship of the World Wide Church,

the courage and wisdom needed to share in building such a world.

                                        Amen.

O Lord our God, we pray for all the churches with which the Church of Scotland is linked in partnership in mission and for all who have gone from Scotland to serve with them.

We remember in particular our

Missionary partner ....

and the church in .... with which he/she is working.

Open our ears to hear what You, Lord, are saying to us through these churches.

We pray for:

the Overseas Council and its staff;

those who minister to expatriate congregations;

those who serve among the Jewish people;

missionaries in training;

those serving abroad through Operation Youthshare.

We pray that there may be men and women ready to respond to the requests from overseas churches for trained personnel. Help us to be faithful and imaginative in making these requests known and to be generous in our support of mission worldwide through the Church's Mission and Service Fund.

We remember the people of different races and faiths who have come to live amongst us. Help us to show loving concern for them. Help us to see how we can give support to those who work among families of overseas backgrounds and with overseas students.

Lord of the Church, we pray that the Church may become more truly Your collective body in the world today the Christ community directed by You, its Head.

Grant that we and all its members may be so filled with Your Holy Spirit that we may be enabled to love and serve our neighbours, near and far.

These things we pray in Jesus' Name,

Amen.

Prayers for a Social Responsibility Meeting

O Living Christ, make us conscious now of Your healing presence,
touch our eyes that we may see You;
open our ears that we may hear Your voice;
enter our hearts that we may truly know You,
and so love You that we may fully serve You,
whom to serve is perfect freedom.

Loving Father, we remember today the work of the Social Responsibility Committee of the Church.

We pray for all within the care of our homes and hostels, rehabilitation centres and List D schools.

We pray for the agents of the Committee in a very demanding work, for that combination of high standards, patient working and ability to comunicate, that are so essential in the healing process they seek.

We remember especially the social workers of the Community Care Section.

We give thanks for the caring, compassionate work of all who give of themselves to further the work of Your church on earth.

In Jesus' name we offer our prayer, Amen.

———

Almighty and Loving Father,
You have given us a new commandment, that we should love one another.
Give us grace that we may fulfil that commandment.
Make us gentle, courteous and forbearing.
Direct our lives so that we may look each to the good of the other, in word and deed.

We give thanks for the church and its caring ministry — for the social workers of the church extending sympathy, understanding, and practical help to all in need.

We thank You for those engaged in the work of counselling development and training, who seek to enable local congregations to be more caring and supportive groups.

We remember before You all who work within our establishments, and pray that You will grant them wisdom, understanding and love in all they seek to do in Your name. Amen.

Prayers suitable for a
Young Woman's Group Meeting

Dear God, bless our homes and make them places of love and laughter.
Help us with the up-bringing of our children that we may guide them along the path which leads to You.

Lord, be near to all who are less happily placed than we are. We think of families who haven't enough to eat and no place to call home. We think of women and children who are victims of violence in their own homes. Help us to be more aware of how we can help such people, for Your love is for all and we must show that love.

Dear Lord, as our children grow older, help us better to understand their needs — and acknowledge our own need. Help us to accept the fact that our children will not always need us, and help us to train them for the time when they must make their own decisions and go their own way. Help us to teach them to seek and follow Your guidance, for if You are with them they will lack nothing.

For give us Lord, the many times we have failed You. We have been impatient and irritable with our families. We have been resentful and grudging of the needs of our children. Help us at such times to be still before You and to count our blessings, that with grateful hearts we may serve You in cring for our families.

Almighty God, we thank You for all grannies and grandpas; for our parents, who have given us so much and who still shower us with love and kindness; for their willingness to look after our children and the love they have for them. Help us to be aware of the anxieties and fears of our parents, especially the fear of not being wanted. Help us to be tolerant and to try to understand that they too have needs. Especially we ask Your blessing on all who have no children nearby to care for them. May we help to take Your love to them. In Christ's name we ask it, Amen.

———

Living Lord, we ask Your blessing upon our families and friends, both here in our group and those scattered around the world. Help us to know that distance is no barrier to You, and that Your love binds us together wherever we may be.

Prayers suitable for a Committee Meeting

Almighty God, Creator of all, we bow before You and praise and thank You for all your goodness to us.
As we meet to discuss and plan the work of our Guild branch, help us to put aside all the duties and demands of this day that have concerned us; help us to think of our members and how, together, we can share the joy of serving You.

Dear Lord, as we meet as a committee of our Woman's Guild,
    guide our thoughts,
    guard our words, and
    grant us the guidance of Your Holy Spirit.

Lord, be present with us as we meet together tonight.
We thank You for the assurance of Your love for each of us, and Your promise to be with us.
We ask for the guidance of Your Holy Spirit in all our business and discussion.
Help us to have open hearts and minds that we may not be afraid of the future and the challenge it presents.
Make us ready to act upon the promptings of Your Spirit that we may go forward, seeking to further Your work in this place and helping those who do Your Work in the far corners of the world.
May we be aware of the needs of the people of the world, and as we plan our syllabus, help us to be ready to learn not only of these needs, but how we can help to meet them.
Thank You Lord, for the privilege of serving you. Forgive us our shortcomings and strengthen us by Your Spirit that we may faithfully follow where You would lead.

Annual General Meeting

Living God, we worship You now, praising You for the past, and trusting You for the future.
We give thanks for the session now ending,
for the joy we have had, the friendship we have known, and the new things we have learned.
Guide us in our choice of office-bearers and committee members tonight.
Make us ready to change our ways when this would make us more effective in Your service.
Help us we pray, to be thoughtful stewards of our money,
so that Your church may be strong to proclaim the good news of Your love, and to develop its care for those in need wherever they may be.
All this we ask in Jesus' name.
                                                      Amen.

Dear Lord, we come to praise and worship You this evening.
How quickly our session has passed!
Thank You for all the joy we have known,
for all we have learned of Your work and of what is happening in the world around us.
We thank You for all those who have served so well during this session,
for the committee members, our pianist, office-bearers and all who have given of themselves to further the work of this branch.
We thank You too for the faithful attendance and support of the members.
We would ask a special blessing on those who have not been well enough to join with us.
Be with us Lord, as we elect our new office - bearers and committee members
May we all be prepared to share the responsibility of running this Guild branch,

doing whatever we can to foster the loving, caring and supportive work of the Woman's Guild.
Guide us as we plan how our funds should be spent.
Help us to be good stewards of what has been entrusted to us.
May all we do and say this night be pleasing to You Lord; in Christ's name, we ask it. Amen.